A Cauldron
of
Good Luck Spells

Little Cauldron of Good Luck Spells

Midia Star

 A GODSFIELD BOOK
www.godsfieldpress.com

This book is dedicated to all those who are
down on their luck right now.

First published in Great Britain in 2004
by Godsfield, a division of
Octopus Publishing Group Ltd
2–4 Heron Quays
Docklands
London E14 4JP

10 9 8 7 6 5 4 3 2 1

Printed and bound in China

ISBN 1 84181 237 4
EAN 9781841812373

Disclaimer
This book is intended to give general information
only. The publisher, author and distributor expressly
disclaim all liability to any person arising directly or
indirectly from the use of, or any errors or omissions
in, the information in this book. The adoption and
application of the information in this book is at the
reader's discretion and is their sole responsibility.

Contents

Introduction

Welcome to this book, which is designed so that you can dip into it whenever you feel the need for a little magick in your life. If you have had a run of bad luck, or feel that you are just being unlucky, pick up this little cauldron of good luck spells and you will find the answer – it's the book every girl should carry in her handbag!

This is a collection of spells and charms guaranteed to help you out when bad luck strikes. I have selected all the spells specifically so that anyone can use this book – there are no expensive ingredients to buy or complicated rituals to perform, and you don't necessarily need to be 'into' magick in order to create a life overflowing with good luck.

The first section is dedicated to spells and charms for bringing good luck into your life, including:

• Luck in love
• Luck in your business

- Luck in your career

- Luck in selling your house

- Luck in the lottery.

The second section is designed for those times when you experience bad luck in your life; it includes spells and charms for:

- Banishing bad luck

- Improving ill health

- Facing up to a legal situation

- Overcoming financial bad luck

- Removing a haunting.

All the spells and charms in this book have been tried and tested and have been personally selected by me. You do not need any hard-to-track-down items or special tools. The main ingredient required with every spell or charm is your belief that it will work. I hope you enjoy working with this little cauldron of spells, and bring good luck flowing into every area of your life.

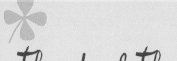

The rules of The Craft

I like to include in my books a small amount of information about spell craftwork and how you should go about it. I know it's tempting to flick straight to the spell offering advice on how to win the lottery, but if you are a beginner in witchcraft it is important to read this bit first. Even if you are familiar with the practices of The Craft, you will find some useful tips in this section, so please take a moment to read it before rushing to the spells.

Although I have no intention of preaching to you, it is important to know a few basic 'house rules' when working with magick. If you try to perform spells without any prior knowledge of how spell crafting works, your spells will either fail to work or will have disastrous consequences. Here are some rules that you should take note of when you apply practical magick to your life.

The Threefold Law

Different magick books give different 'rules', but every book you read about spell craft will tell you about the Threefold Law. This is the most important rule that you will learn and is not solely applicable to witches – it is the way of the universe. You've doubtless heard the saying 'Luck comes in threes'. Well, there is truth in this saying – whatever you give out comes back to you three times. In fact, it can come back to you up to seven times! If you do something that is regarded as unpleasant to another person or living thing, then it will come back to you at some point in your life, and never as you would have imagined. The same applies if you do something beneficial to another person – your kindness will be rewarded.

Please don't panic after reading about the Threefold Law and think that because you accidentally spilled coffee on your boss's computer, you will be damned for eternity – or, at the very least, will have seven lots of bad luck! Accidents happen, and they don't count. It's your *true* intention that is important. If you intentionally poured coffee all over your boss's laptop, then that's a different matter altogether, and at some point in your life you will suffer because of it. This is not just something that applies to witchcraft – it's the way life is, I'm afraid.

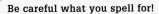

Be careful what you spell for!

There's an old saying: 'Be careful what you wish for, as it just might come true.' This is a golden rule to stick by when you are spell casting. Spells are powerful, and they do work. So, whenever you decide to do a spell, think carefully about what you really want. You might desire a complete change of luck in your career. Say you were an out-of-work actress and desperately wanted your big break, could you handle working seven nights a week on Broadway, never having a day off? And what if Hollywood suddenly snapped you up? Could you cope with the press intrusion? I'm not saying you shouldn't follow your dreams, but do

think about the consequences of a spell before you perform it, because spells make things happen.

If you perform a spell and later regret doing it, don't worry – you can always retract it. I'll show you how to do this at the end of the book (see pages 120–123).

Tools of the trade

This is my favourite controversial topic, and one that receives a lot of debate where spell crafters are concerned. There are many books out there that will tell you that you *must* have an array of 'witchy wonders' in order to do 'real' witchcraft. My answer? Don't believe all you read! Magick is for everyone – regardless of sex, colour, age or religion – and not just for members of an elite club.

It's not necessary to purchase a wand, have an altar or an array of witchy gadgets. Likewise, you don't have to own a wardrobe full of black cloaks and pointed hats. You can craft spells using no tools whatsoever, except for the tool within you – the power of your mind.

Many people can't afford all the gadgets that are available to perform practical magick, and others wish to keep their interest in magick quiet from family and friends – and advertising the fact by painting a big pentagram on your front door would soon put paid to that!

If you really want to buy some of the 'tools of the trade', then go ahead, but it is not a necessary part of spell work. Our magickal ancestors couldn't pop into the nearest New Age store and buy a crystal ball or a collection of mystical gadgets. They had to rely on what was free and readily available from nature to enhance their spells. I intentionally use spells that do not require expensive or hard-to-find ingredients, and I certainly don't tell readers to go out and buy a collection of 'witchy toys'.

The power of the moon

It's a fact: the moon has a great influence on our lives. Have you ever noticed how at certain times of the month you are more irritable or happier than at other times? This is because the gravitational pull that the moon exerts on the Earth not only affects our tides and weather, but our behaviour too.

The word 'lunacy' comes from *luna*, the Latin word for the moon, and studies have shown that the moon is a significant trigger in instances of mental illness, particularly when the moon is full.

When we perform magick at different times of the month, it has different results:

• The time when the moon is waxing (when it looks like a D-shape in the sky, in the period leading up to a full moon) is the best time to perform spells for gaining things, such as a new job.

• The waning moon (when it looks like a C-shape, in the period between the full and new moon) is an ideal time to banish things from your life, such as a run of bad luck.

• The new moon, or dark moon as it's sometimes called (when you can't see the moon in the sky), is a time for new beginnings and for banishing old habits and burying the past.

• The full moon is a time for getting results and gaining things in your life.

It is not imperative that you do a spell on a certain moon phase, but it does give your spell more power if you do. Your diary or calendar should tell you what phase the moon is in, or you can buy moon-phase charts in most New Age shops. As a general rule, if I intend to do a spell and the moon is not in the right phase, then I will wait until it is. If it's an emergency, you can perform the spell if the moon isn't in the correct phase, but you will need to work harder at it.

The power of fire

Candles represent the fire element in our world and play an important part in spell crafting, and this is one of the reasons why you will find many candle spells in this book. It is widely believed – and has been proved – that certain days combined with specific coloured candles can enhance a spell, speed it up and make it more powerful. When dealing with luck spells, try to use silver, gold, green or orange-coloured candles. But if you can't find the correct colour of candle for a particular spell, you can always use a normal white household candle, which is easy to obtain from any household store or supermarket.

The best days for good luck magick are:

- Monday – spells for matters to do with the home
- Tuesday – spells for protection
- Wednesday – spells to do with the way you think
- Thursday – spells for business matters or the law
- Friday – for affairs of the heart
- Saturday – spells for banishing things from your life
- Sunday – for confidence and success; for example, if you need extra confidence for an interview.

However, it is not essential to do a certain spell on a certain day, with a particular coloured candle, under a specific moon phase. If you want to do a spell and don't have the suggested ingredients, then improvise. The spells in this book are those that have worked for me or for people whom I know. The best spells are the ones that come from inside you. So long as you believe in magick and respect it, it will work for you.

We can now get on with the art of spell crafting to bring good luck into your life. But try to remember the points I have included in this section – you may need to refer to them from time to time when doing some of the spells in this book.

Spells and charms for good luck

We always assume that whenever good things happen unexpectedly in our lives, it is all down to luck. How many times have you heard people say, 'You lucky thing' or 'That was a stroke of luck'?

People who are positive by nature, and who believe in themselves and their dreams, live healthier and fuller lives and appear to get all the 'lucky breaks' by being in the right place at the right time. Conversely, people who appear always to be down on their luck, or who experience run after run of bad luck, tend to be negative by nature and expect bad things to happen to them. The key factor in both types of people is the power of the mind – it's the basic principle of cause and effect. If you convince yourself that you are unlucky, then you will attract bad luck to you; if you convince yourself that you are lucky, then you will attract good luck.

Magick and belief work hand-in-hand. If you don't believe that a spell will work for you, then no amount of throwing herbs to the four corners of the Earth will make it do so. The power of magick requires one important tool – your belief. With practice, you can learn the art of the old Craft, but if you don't believe in it, you won't achieve the results you desire. Even if you feel you have been the unluckiest person on the planet, you can put the past to rest and be assured that, by following the instructions given in this book and by really believing that your luck will change, it will. You *can* have endless amounts of good luck flowing into your life.

This section is dedicated to bringing you good luck – whether that is a boost of luck in your career or luck in love. Once you combine the ingredients of a spell with a small amount of belief, you will be able to have luck in every area of your life. If you do suffer a stroke of bad luck, all you need do is find the spell for your particular problem, and – hey presto! – you will send the bad luck back where it came from.

A complete change in luck

This is a ritual for when you feel as though the whole world is against you – it's probably not, you know, but it may feel like that sometimes. If you think you need a complete change of luck in every area of your life, try this powerful candle spell.

You will need

One long green candle

A silver pin

A green ballpoint pen

Matches or a lighter

What you do

Start this spell on a Friday, ideally when the moon is full.

Sometimes you might have to wait a full 28 days in order to do this spell on a full moon. If you can't wait for the full moon, don't worry too much – you should see the same results – but do try to start the spell on a Friday night.

You need to keep this spell going for nine days in total for it to have its full effect, so make sure that you can leave your candle in a safe place where it won't be disturbed.

First of all, divide the candle into nine equal parts by marking a horizontal line with the silver pin eight times down the stem of the candle. There should be about 2.5cm (1in) between each line, but obviously this depends on the size of your candle.

After doing this, close your eyes and stick the pin into the candle. It doesn't matter where – that's up to you. Next take your green pen and inscribe the word 'Luck' in each of the nine segments you have created.

Ideally, on the first night of the full moon, leave your inscribed candle out in the garden or on a windowsill so that it catches full moonlight for one whole night. The following night light the candle and say the following words six times:

> *Lord and Lady,*
> *hear my plea*
> *Make my fortune*
> *change for me*
> *Banish now my*
> *past misfortune*
> *And return good luck*
> *this full moon.*

Allow the first segment of the candle to burn down and then blow it out. Bow to the moon three times. Repeat this process for the next eight nights. When the pin falls from the candle, this is the sign that your bad luck has ended. If you have any wax left after the nine days, bury it in your garden. You should soon notice an improvement in your luck in general.

21

Lucky winning charm

Don't get too excited – this charm will not guarantee a huge win when gambling. Sorry! It will, however, increase your chances of winning if you play the lottery, enter competitions or gamble. We live in a world where the universe provides us with everything we need. When we think about it, few us actually *need* a win on the lottery. Yes, we could all do with some extra cash from time to time, but magick works best when there is a genuine need for something in our lives. However, the Goddess likes a little flutter from time to time too, and so long as you don't abuse her powers, she will help you to boost your income with this lucky winning charm.

You will need

A piece of green card

A green pen

One silver coin

Sticky tape

Clear adhesive acrylic

What you do

Do this spell on a Friday night.

It's not very likely that you will be able to find a lucky four-leafed clover in a hurry, so you are going to make one yourself – this will give it added magickal luck, because it comes directly from you.

First of all, draw a four-leafed clover on the piece of card with your green pen. It needs to be small enough to fit in your purse or wallet. Tape the silver coin to the back of the clover leaf and write around the coin the words 'Lottery Luck' as many times as space will permit. Then cover it with the clear adhesive acrylic. This is to keep the coin clean and protected.

Depending on whether you are right- or left-handed, hold the clover in your more dominant hand and close your eyes. Visualize pushing luck power into the palm of your hand. As you do this you should feel your palm becoming warm. When you feel ready, say the following words three times:

Lady Luck
shine on me
Help me with the lottery.
I am not starved,
I am not greedy
Bring me luck when
I am needy.

When you buy your next lottery ticket, wrap it round the four-leafed clover until it is time to check your numbers. If you are using your lucky clover for a competition, place the charm on top of the entry form while you fill out your name and address. For any other purpose, such as visiting a casino, carry it with you when you buy your chips. And always carry your four-leafed clover in your purse or wallet at other times. If you haven't used your lucky charm for a while, recharge it by repeating the incantation three times.

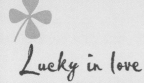

Lucky in love

As the old saying goes, 'Love rarely runs smoothly.' But you *can* be lucky in love – you just need a little helping hand with a bit of practical magick from time to time. Try this love spell to attract the good guys to you and keep the bad boys away.

You will need

One rose-scented candle
  (or one pink candle and
  some rose oil)
Matches or a lighter
One rose incense stick
A recent photograph of yourself

What you do

Do this spell on a waxing moon, and at midnight on a Friday if you can.

At the stroke of midnight, light your candle. If you can't find a rose-scented one, you can use a pink candle and anoint it with rose oil. Light the incense stick and hold it in your left hand. Hold the photograph of yourself in your right hand and waft the incense smoke clockwise round the photograph, saying the following words:

Goddess Venus, hear my plea
Stop attracting
bad guys to me
Bring me good guys
from now on
So I can pick from one
of them.
This is my request
to you above
Make me feel lucky in love.

Allow the candle and incense stick to burn away, and place the photograph on your windowsill for 28 nights.

27

Lucky crystal talisman

A talisman is simply an item that a person believes to be lucky. Talismans have been around for hundreds of years, and whether it's a lucky rabbit's foot or a special coin, if the owner believes it is lucky, then it will be. Crystals hold their own special magickal power, and this talisman is created using a crystal to give it extra magickal luck. Carry this charm with you whenever you need some luck in your life.

You will need

One crystal (as large or as small as you can find or afford)

50ml (2fl oz) bottled water

Two drops each of the following oils: rose, lavender and tea tree

What you do

You can do this spell at any time.

This is a really easy, but very powerful, spell. Take the crystal and wash it thoroughly in the bottled water. This completely cleanses it and takes away any negative energy that it may have picked up in the place where you found or bought it. Put two drops of each oil onto the crystal and gently rub them in. When you have done this, hold the crystal in your cupped hands and say six times:

Lucky crystal
By your power
bring me your luck.

Keep your crystal in a safe place in your home. When the smell of the oils disappears, do the spell again. Remember to cleanse the crystal first.

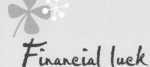

Financial luck

As I mentioned earlier in the Lucky Winning Charm (see pages 22–25), the universe provides us with what we need – and that includes sufficient money for our needs. But if you find that you have more bills than salary, try this little money-luck spell. Remember: all spells work best when there is a genuine need, so don't be greedy or do this spell just for the sake of it. If you *really need* some extra cash, this spell will work.

You will need

A note of your own currency

One green candle

Five peppermint leaves

Five silver coins

Some salt water (two teaspoons of salt to 50ml/2fl oz of water)

Matches or a lighter

A cup of boiled water

What you do

You should do this spell on a Friday or a full moon.

First of all, place the paper money under your green candle. (If you really are that broke that you don't have a note, don't worry – you can always raid the kids' Monopoly set, or even draw your own money.) Arrange the five peppermint leaves round the base of the candle in a circle. Next, wash the silver coins in the salt water to cleanse any negativity from them, and then place one coin on top of each mint leaf. Light the candle, and say the following words five times:

Oh Money Lord
Hear my plea
Send some money
on to me.
Look my way,
look my way
Hear my plea and
brighten my day
Thank you, so mote it be.

Allow the candle to burn down. Then take the mint leaves and place them in a cup of boiled water, allowing them to brew for five minutes. Take the leaves out and sip the peppermint tea. The leaves will have absorbed the magick that you put into them, and will in turn be absorbed back into you.

Keep the coins in your purse or wallet along with the note that you placed under the candle. Allow the mint leaves to dry out, then crush them and throw them out of the window. This signifies that the spell is complete.

Did you know?

We all know that a horseshoe is supposed to be lucky, but do you know why? The U-shape of the horseshoe is the most powerful sign of protection, and any bad luck thrown to a U-shape will simply rebound to the original source. A horseshoe is nailed with seven nails, and seven is one of the luckiest numbers around. To receive luck from a horseshoe, it must be found, not purchased. And, according to the Greeks and Romans, the horseshoe should be placed over a doorway.

A lucky audition

I have tried to include a mixture of gook luck spells in this book, so that it applies to people with very different lifestyles. This spell is for you if you are in the entertainment industry and are attending auditions. You might be an aspiring actor, a musician or a vocalist. Whichever is the case, try this spell for success at your next audition – just remember me when you're signed up by some Hollywood producer!

You will need

A piece of gold card

Scissors

A pen

Silver sequins

Glue

One gold candle

One silver candle

1m (1yd) thin gold ribbon

Matches or a lighter

What you do

Do this spell on a Sunday night or a full moon.

Cut a large star shape out of the piece of gold card and, in the centre of it, write your name. Stick silver sequins all round the edge of the star so that it glitters. Place your star on a windowsill or a table, then put the gold candle to the left of the star and the silver candle to the right. Place the thin gold ribbon in front of the star. Light both candles and say the following:

Star light, Star bright
Grant my wish
for me tonight.
Stardom beckons just for me
Grant this wish,
so mote it be.

Allow both candles to burn down. Stick the gold star to the door of your bedroom and imagine this as your dressing-room door. Visualize, as far as you can, how life will be when you become a star – signing autographs, attending premieres, bowing to your audience, and so on.

The spell is now complete. The only thing you need to remember, when you go for an audition, is to take the piece of gold ribbon along with you. While you are waiting to be auditioned, hold the ribbon in your hands and tie 13 random knots in it. If you have a long time to wait, undo the knots one by one and tie them again, until it is time for you to be seen. Keep visualizing getting through the audition successfully and how life as a celebrity will be for you. The ribbon will not only take your mind off your nerves – it acts as a magickal cord that will transfer to your audition the magick that you set up in the spell.

37

Interview luck

This is an old, tried-and-tested spell that I have suggested many times for people who need success at an interview – all of them have either secured the job they have been going for or been promoted. It is therefore also suitable if you are going for promotion at your current place of work.

You will need

A matchbox

A pinch of chopped mint

A pinch of chopped rosemary

A pinch of mixed spice

A pinch of cinnamon

One small silver coin

Some salt water (two teaspoons of salt to 50ml/2fl oz of water)

One small piece of blue giftwrap

A piece of blue ribbon

One blue candle

Matches or a lighter

What you do

You should do this spell the night before your interview.

Blue is the colour of luck in the workplace, so it is advisable to wear something blue if you are going for an interview or attending a work appraisal. This could be in your clothing or something small, such as a handkerchief or even a blue garter under your skirt.

Prepare this spell the night before you go to your interview. Open the matchbox and place all the herbs and spices inside it. Wash the silver coin in the salted water to cleanse any negativity from it, then place it in the matchbox. Next, wrap the matchbox up in the giftwrap so that it looks like a mini-parcel. Tie the blue ribbon round it and secure it. Light the blue candle and say the following three times:

My door to the future
is open wide
Your light will guide
the way for me
And show me the path to
a better future
Where more money and
fulfilment await me.

Allow the blue candle to burn down. Before you go to bed, shake the matchbox three times and then sleep with it under your pillow. Prior to your interview the following morning, shake the box again three times. You should sail through with flying colours. However, if you don't get the job, don't panic – it doesn't mean the spell hasn't worked; it simply means this particular job is not for you and that a better one is nearby.

Did you know?

We all like to dabble with a bit of eye-shadow on our eyelids from time to time, but did you know that it was first thought of by the Egyptians to bring luck and protect against the Devil? They would decorate their eyelids with colour, so that when they were asleep, it looked as though they were in fact awake and scared the Devil away.

41

A lucky influence

It's possible to influence someone without their knowing about it, and this spell is designed to do just that. Use this spell wisely, though – don't try to influence everyone you come across, because magick isn't the easy solution to everything.

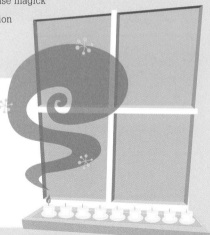

You will need

One sheet of gold or
  yellow paper

Scissors

A pen

Nine gold tea-lights

Matches or a lighter

What you do

Start this nine-day spell on a Sunday.

Cut the sheet of gold or yellow paper lengthways, about 5cm (2in) in, so that you have a long strip of paper. On this write the name of the person you wish to influence and what you wish the outcome of your quest to be. Place the nine gold tea-lights on top of the strip of paper on a windowsill, or somewhere else they won't be moved, because this spell needs to be left undisturbed for the full nine days.

On the Sunday that you start the spell, light the first tea-light and say the following words nine times:

[Name of person],
you shall grant my desire
You shall grant my wish
Your power cannot resist.
By the power of
this fire
You shall grant my desire
So mote it be.

Allow the tea-light to burn down and then leave it. The following eight nights perform the same ritual until all the tea-lights have burned down. You should hear soon from the person you are trying to influence.

Lucky gnome

Tradition has it that gnomes are mischievous little things. They are magickal little things, too! You can release the magick from the humble gnome by performing this ritual in your garden – you will soon see how much luck your gnome brings you.

You will need

One garden gnome

100ml (3½fl oz) salt water
(four teaspoons of salt to
100ml/3½fl oz water)

A name for your gnome

A handful of gold glitter

What you do

Do this spell on a full moon.

First, cleanse your gnome by washing him in half of the salt water. Next, take your gnome out into the garden and place him or her in a spot where you like to sit. When you have thought of a nice name for your gnome (mine's Hamish, by the way), gently pour the remaining salt water over him. Before the water dries, sprinkle the gold glitter all over your gnome, so that it sticks to his body. Gently blow any remaining glitter from the gnome and repeat the following words three times:

By the magick of three
I give life to thee.
When I pat you three
You will bring luck
to me.

You have now released the power of magick in your gnome. Every time you need a little extra luck in your life, pat your lucky gnome three times and your wish will be granted.

A lucky home

Some homes are said to be unlucky, but no one wants to live in a place where bad luck comes and goes all the time. This spell will encourage luck in your home. After doing it, you should notice a difference in the atmosphere.

You will need

Five sprigs of rosemary

Five sprigs of parsley

Five sprigs of lavender

1m (1yd) green ribbon

What you do

Do this spell on a Monday or a waning moon, if possible.

Let the herbs dry out by placing them in a warm oven (110°C/225°F) or an airing cupboard. When they are dry, gather them all together and tie them in a bunch using the green ribbon. Don't cut off any of the ribbon – leave it trailing from the bunch of herbs, as this will encourage good luck into your home.

Place the bunch of herbs above your doorway, and say the following:

*Only good luck may pass
through this house
Bad luck is not permitted.
My Lord and Lady,
encourage the flow of
good luck
To our home.*

When your lucky herbs are looking a bit tired, repeat the spell using a fresh collection of herbs.

Luck in selling your home

In the ever-changing housing climate you can always do with a bit of luck in selling your home. This little ritual will help the sale of your property to run smoothly.

You will need

One crystal

Some salt water (two teaspoons of salt to 50ml/2fl oz of water)

A photograph of the front of your property (get this from your estate agent)

One white candle

Matches or a lighter

What you do

Do this spell for six days, starting on a Monday or a full moon.

First, you need to cleanse your crystal by soaking it in the salt water. Leave the crystal in the solution while you prepare the rest of the spell.

Find a place, such as a windowsill, where your candle can remain undisturbed. Place the photograph of your house under the white candle, then light the candle. Say the following three times:

*My home is available
to you now
I no longer need it
Come and see.
This happy home is
calling to you
May you desire it to
be your home
So mote it be.*

Blow the candle out and reuse it over the next five days, repeating the incantation each time. Then dry the crystal and place it in a prominent part of your house. When prospective buyers come to view your house, the crystal will emit this positive energy to them.

Luck in buying a property

This spell will help you find the home that is most suited to you and secure your finances so that you are able to buy it.

You will need

Three orange candles

One small toy house (available from most toy stores)

Three mint leaves

Three sprigs of lavender

Matches or a lighter

What you do

Do this spell on a Friday, a Monday or a waxing moon.

Arrange the three candles round the toy house. Place the mint leaves and the sprigs of lavender close to the house. Light the three candles, moving in a clockwise direction.

As the flames rise, visualize your dream home or property being available to you. It doesn't matter if you don't have the necessary funds right now – try not to think about that. Imagine that you have the power to create the finances you need to buy the property you want. Visualize phoning the removal men to pack up your old home, and arriving at your new dream home.

Imagine putting the key in the front door of your new house, walking in and feeling instantly at home.

When you feel you can visualize no more, leave the room and allow the candles to burn safely down. Keep your toy house, mint and lavender wherever you keep your house keys. You will soon notice something happening that will enable you to buy your new home.

Business Luck

This spell is designed to create an increase in luck for
your business.

You will need

One sheet of white card

A pen

Four silver stars
(available from most stationers)

Glue

One silver coin

What you do

Do this spell on a Thursday evening or a waxing moon.

The first thing you need to do is write down all the things you want for your business. More clients? More money? More time off? To open your own shop? To work from home? Think in the future tense and visualize how you want your business to be within the next couple of years. Whatever you want, write it down on the piece of card.

Stick one silver star in each corner of the card. Then stick the silver coin on the reverse of the card. Close your eyes and say the following:

*This manifesto represents
the wishes for my business
May you, Lord and Lady,
grant me my wishes
May you manifest
my dreams
And make the
written word reality
So mote it be.*

Keep your piece of card in a safe place wherever you work – for example, in your desk or with your work equipment. You will now attract opportunities that will in turn grant your wishes. Soon you will be ticking off the desires listed on your business luck card.

Travel luck

If you travel a lot, this is the perfect charm to take with you to ensure that you have a safe and lucky trip – a traveller should never be without it.

You will need

Four sticks about 7.5cm (3in) in length

Two sprigs of lavender

1m (1yd) green ribbon

Three drops of lavender oil

What you do

Make this charm on a Thursday.

Arrange the four sticks in the shape of a compass (see illustration).

Lay the two sprigs of lavender on top of two of the sticks that cross at the centre of the compass. Then take the piece of green ribbon and tie the sticks and the lavender together, so that it really looks like a compass.

Anoint the compass with the lavender oil, and say the following:

Archangel Raphael
Bless this charm with your protection
And protect me when I journey
From north to south and east to west
Guide me so that I travel and return safely.

Whenever you have to travel, take your lucky charm with you. When travelling in your car, keep a spare length of ribbon and hang the charm somewhere it will not distract you. When the fragrance of lavender disappears, re-anoint the compass and repeat the words of the spell.

A lucky career

If you would like a change of luck in your career, use this spell, which is designed to increase the number of opportunities you have to get ahead in your profession.

You will need

Three bay leaves

A pebble

A gold pen

One gold candle

Matches or a lighter

What you do

You should do this spell on a Sunday or a full moon.

Arrange the three bay leaves to form a triangle shape. Write the word *'luck'* on the pebble with the gold pen and place it in the centre of the triangle. Put the gold candle behind the arrangement and light it. Say the following three times:

By this golden light
Make my career bright
Send me golden opportunities
To lighten my life.

Allow the candle to burn down. Throw the bay leaves and any remaining wax away. Place the pebble in your purse, wallet or handbag. Whenever you remember, rub the pebble for increased luck.

Did you know?

You've doubtless heard the theory that if you break a mirror, you will receive seven years' bad luck. But do you know why? The mirror was considered by the Romans to be the tool of the gods because, when man saw his reflection in a lake or a pond, he thought he was seeing his soul. The Romans were responsible for adding the seven years' bad luck rule. To break the bad luck, you should sweep up the pieces of mirror and bury them in the garden.

Lucky pet spell

Cats are said to be lucky enough to have nine lives, but what about all the other living creatures we adopt as our pets? This spell will ensure that your cat, dog, hamster or even your goldfish enjoys a healthy, lucky life.

You will need

One rose-scented candle

One feather

One rose incense stick and holder (or secure the stick with a small piece of removable adhesive)

Something to represent your pet (a collar, feeding bowl, photograph)

Matches or a lighter

What you do

Do this spell on a Tuesday or a new (dark) moon.

This is an outdoor spell, so you need to do it on a day when it's not going to rain, or the water will extinguish the candle. Find a nice quiet spot in the garden and arrange the objects as follows: place the candle in the centre; put the feather behind the candle; place the incense stick and holder in front of the candle; put the item that represents your pet in front of the incense stick.

Light the candle, then the incense stick, and say the following words:

Goddess, Creator of nature
May you hear my call.
Protect [name of pet] and
all living creatures
No harm may come to all
So mote it be.

Allow the candle to burn down. Wave the object that represents your pet through the smoke of the rose-scented incense and do the same with the feather. Your pet should always be lucky and protected in life from now on.

Luck in pregnancy

It's always a worrying time when you're expecting a child. It doesn't matter if it's your first, second, third or even sixth pregnancy – there's always some concern at the back of your mind when you are pregnant. This pregnancy garland is designed to be hung either in your own bedroom or in your baby's nursery.

You will need

One circle of plain flower oasis (available from florists)

Some dried flowers, holly, twigs, cones, and so on

A few drops of lavender oil

A few drops of jasmine oil

A few drops of orange oil

1m (1yd) white ribbon

One green candle

Matches or a lighter

What you do

Make this charm on a full moon.

Take the flower oasis and insert the dried flowers, holly, twigs and cones into it, so that the whole circle is covered in natural produce. The items I have suggested are my own personal choice, but what you select is entirely up to you. Sprinkle drops of each oil over the garland. Then wind the ribbon evenly round the garland so that it looks pretty.

Place the green candle in the centre of the garland. Light the candle, place both of your hands on your stomach and say the following words:

Diana,
goddess of fertility
May you protect this new
life of mine.
Allow this new life to grow
into a healthy child
Bless him/her with the
strength to grow
Until we meet.
This is my wish,
so mote it be.

Allow the candle to burn down and then hang your pregnancy garland up in the room of your choice. You will have a safe and happy pregnancy.

A lucky child

We all want our children to be lucky in life. This spell will
draw luck into your child's life, where it will stay for evermore.

You will need

A few drops of lavender oil

A bunch of dried flowers

Some tissue paper

What you do

Do this spell whenever you get a rare moment alone.

Sprinkle the lavender oil on the dried flowers, then place the flowers on your child's pillow. Kneel down, as if saying a prayer, and repeat the following:

*As the mother to my child,
I dedicate my life to him/her
I endeavour to protect
him/her in so far
as in my power.
Help him/her to be lucky
and protected in life*

*At times when I may not be
here for him/her
Bless his/her path of life
with luck and love
And his/her life will be
always and for ever
happy and safe.*

Visualize for as long as time will permit the image of your child with a warm orange glow surrounding him or her. When you have finished, wrap the flowers up in some tissue paper and store them in a safe place. Sprinkle a few drops of the lavender oil onto your child's pillow. Your child will be lucky from now on.

Luck in health

Good health can't be bought, no matter how much money you
have, so it's always handy to have a little spell to keep you in
tip-top condition. This one makes a refreshing cup of tea
packed with magickal feel-better ingredients. The spell is
intended as a helping hand to keep you in good health – not
as an alternative to going to see the doctor.

You will need

A cup of boiled water

One green-tea teabag (available from
supermarkets or health-food stores)

One teaspoon of honey

One mint leaf

One bay leaf

What you do

Do this whenever you feel unwell, or to encourage good health.

Boil a cupful of water and allow it to cool slightly. Place the teabag in the water and leave it to brew for five minutes. Take the teabag out and stir in the teaspoon of honey. Place the mint leaf and bay leaf in the cup and leave for another five minutes. Then hold your hands round the cup and say the following:

*Lord and Lady
of the universe
May you bring me
good health
May you keep illness away
And disease at bay
Thank you, so mote it be.*

Take the mint and bay leaves out and then sip your cup of goodness. Green-tea helps to aid digestion, while the honey will give your immune system a boost, the mint leaf will promote a prosperous life and the bay leaf will keep illness at bay.

Luck in exams

This is an ideal spell to perform if you, or someone you know, has an exam coming up. This might be anything from a driving test to the final exams of a degree course.

You will need

One gold candle

One cinnamon incense stick

Matches or a lighter

A small purse or pouch

What you do

Do this spell on a Wednesday.

Find a time and a quiet place where you will not be disturbed for half an hour. Light the gold candle and the incense stick and close your eyes. Imagine yourself sitting in the room where you are to take your exam or test. Concentrate on your breathing and listen as you breathe in and out. When you inhale, try to breathe from your stomach, rather than your chest.

Imagine yourself being completely relaxed and able to pass this exam or test with ease. Imagine you have done the test many times and can easily pass it. When you are satisfied that you have visualized enough,

allow the candle to burn down until there is 2.5cm (1in) of wax left. Place the remaining wax in your purse or pouch. You need to take this with you when you go for your test or exam.

Just before your exam, allow ten minutes to visualize the same images you created when you started the spell. Tell yourself that you have passed your test and that you are just going through the necessary steps to gain that certificate or licence. Make sure you concentrate on your breathing and, above all, remain relaxed.

67

Luck in marriage

The union of two people by marriage is intended to last for life, and we could all do with an extra bit of marital luck, just to make sure everything runs smoothly. This spell will bring luck to any marriage, regardless of what life throws at you.

You will need

One green candle

Two drops of rose oil

Two pink rose petals

Matches or a lighter

What you do

Start this nine-day spell on Friday or a waxing moon.

First of all, anoint the green candle with the rose oil and rub it into the candle. Place the two rose petals on either side of the candle: one represents you and the other your partner. Light the candle, and say the following words six times:

Lady Venus, goddess of love
May you bring harmony
and love to this marriage
Grant us a happy union
for life
Grant us joy and peace

May any troubles quietly
pass us by.
Make this be the greatest
love of all
And allow only happiness
for evermore.

Blow the candle out after doing this spell. Keep the candle in the same place and repeat the ritual at the same time every day for the next eight days.

When you finish the spell, bury any remaining wax in your garden and throw the rose petals up in the air to the south, so that they are carried to the universe by the wind. Your marriage should now be filled with luck and love for evermore.

Musical luck

This spell is for anyone who aspires to a career in the music industry. This might be as a successful singer, working behind the scenes promoting bands, or in a large orchestra.

You will need

One small amethyst

One sprig of rosemary

One oak leaf

One green candle

Matches or a lighter

Something that represents your musical talent (for example, a guitar or a song sheet)

What you do

Do this spell on a Thursday or during a full moon.

Place the amethyst, rosemary and oak leaf next to the green candle. Light the candle and hold the item that represents your musical talent in your hands. Imagine for a minute already possessing the luck you need in order to achieve your dreams.

If your dream is to play in an orchestra, visualize how you feel playing with your fellow members. If you aspire to write songs for other people, imagine receiving confirmation that your song is going to be played by your favourite artist. Spend as long as you like dreaming your dream.

When you have finished, say the following words six times:

Talented am I
Rhythm comes from
within me
Musical talent I have
Everyone will share
the same view.
I will reach my dream
So mote it be.

Allow the candle to burn away. Keep the other ingredients with your instrument or with something connected with your music.

Luck in writing

If you are an aspiring writer, but are a bit down on your luck in getting anyone to notice you, this is the spell for you. Remember: magick can only assist you; it won't write a bestselling novel for you – only you can do that. It will, however, help you get your work noticed.

You will need

One long natural-coloured feather

A craft knife

A photocopied sample of your handwriting

One pink candle

Matches or a lighter

What you do

Do this spell on a full moon.

First, you need carefully to shape the bottom of the feather into a point, using the craft knife, so that it looks like a quill. Next, lay the sample of your writing on the desk or table at which you write. (Make sure that you use a photocopy because you are going to bury it.) Place the pink candle on top of the paper and the feather in front of the candle. Light the candle, and say the following words three times:

The pen is mightier than the sword
This quill represents my pen
My strength gives me perseverance
To continue in my quest.
My words on paper are carried to the universe
For all to read
My words are appreciated
My words are enjoyed
So mote it be.

Allow the candle to burn down. Take any remaining wax, the quill and your written sample and, if possible, bury them in the ground.

Finding something lost

It can be so annoying to realize that you've lost something important to you. I've found missing car keys, lost documents, money and endless other family items using this spell.

You will need

One red apple

One green apple

A knife

0.5m (½yd) green ribbon

One green candle

Matches or a lighter

What you do

You should do this spell on a Sunday or a full moon.

Cut the red apple in half, then cut the green apple in half. Pair up the opposite colours, so that you have one apple that is half-red and half-green. Tie the apple together with the green ribbon. Light the green candle, and say the following only once:

*By the powers of
the universe
Come search the land
and sea
For what belongs to me.
Show me the path
to what I seek*

*And in return I offer this
gift so sweet.*

Bury the apple in the garden and eat the other two halves. Now forget all about the lost item – it will turn up when you least expect it.

Did you know?

The rabbit's foot was always considered to be a powerful and lucky charm and a protector against evil. Rabbits are born with their eyes wide open, and it was believed that this meant they could see evil approaching, before anything else could see it.

Specific luck

It would be impossible for me to try and think of every situation where you might need a good luck spell, but I have tried to cover most eventualities. However, if I haven't touched upon a specific situation for which you need a bit of luck, you can always try this lucky spell instead.

You will need

Either the seed from a thistle bush or a white
 feather (natural-coloured, if possible)

What you do

You can perform this spell at any time you like.

In England there is a lovely thistle bush that emits small, white fluffy seeds, which blow through the air during the summer. Traditional folklore states that these are nature's fairies, sent to grant us wishes. It is said that if you manage to catch one and whisper your wish to it, then let it go, your wish will be granted. If you are lucky enough to find one of these thistle seeds, catch it, close your eyes and make your lucky wish.

If you don't have one of these little fairies, you can do exactly the same with a white feather. Make your wish

to it, then blow it into the universe and your wish will soon come true.

Did you know?

The Druids were the first to believe in the power of the four-leafed clover. The pretty little weed is in fact a freak of nature – the more common type being the three-leafed variety. Because it is rare to find a four-leafed clover, it is considered very lucky if you do so.

Banishing bad luck

This section deals with banishing bad luck from your life for good. You may notice that you get weeks, sometimes months, when everything seems to go wrong at the same time: the washing machine packs up, your son goes down with chickenpox and you lose your job, all in the same week. These aren't coincidences – it means you are having a run of bad luck. The reason could be one of many. You might have intentionally hurt someone's feelings; you might be feeling negative or be surrounded by negative people – remember that what you send out, you create in reality. You might be the victim of someone cursing you. Don't believe that it's only witches and gypsies who can place a hex on you; anyone and everyone has the ability to do this. They might not know that they are directing bad luck at you, but the mere fact that someone thinks ill of you will transcend the universe and find its target – you.

You might be the most positive person in the world and still seem to attract bad luck over and over again. First, consider if there is someone who is silently inflicting this on you: are you being influenced by negative people? I have an old school friend who is negative about every aspect of life – I only have to spend an hour with her and I come away feeling depressed and fed up with everything in my own life.

If you are in a job, a relationship or a situation that you hate, this in turn will attract bad luck. If you're not following your true path, this could be the reason why you are attracting bad luck.

All the spells in this section should, whenever possible, be performed on a waning or new (dark) moon. Tuesday is the day on which most spells of protection should be performed; Saturday is the day to confuse an enemy; and Sunday is the day for persuasion. If you have experienced a run of bad luck recently, I would suggest that you do an appropriate banishing spell first, followed by a spell from Part One to bring good luck back into your life.

Losing your job

Long gone are the days when you can be in a secure job for the rest of your working life. Nowadays job security is a thing of the past. Even though we are made aware of this every day, it can still be a shock to discover that you have been laid off. It's not the end of the world, though. Banish the bad luck that has caused you to lose your job by performing this simple spell, then turn back to Part One and perform a spell to change your luck from bad to good – or do the Business Luck spell (see pages 52–53).

You will need

Your old employment contract

A red pen

A pinch of black pepper

One black candle

Matches or a lighter

What you do

Do this spell on a waning moon.

Find a time when you can be alone with your thoughts for ten minutes. Open up your old employment contract and draw red lines right through every page. Then sprinkle a pinch of black pepper over it, and fold it up four times. Light the black candle, and say the following words six times:

My bad luck will leave
I banish you to
the depths
This is now in the past
And I am ready
to start afresh.

Wait until the candle has burned right down and, just before it extinguishes itself, pour a few drops of hot wax onto the contract to seal it. The following day bury it right away from your house.

Unemployment spell

Being unemployed can be one of the most stressful situations you ever face, and it can make you feel depressed and disillusioned with life. If you have been unemployed for a while, do this spell to banish unemployment from your life. As suggested previously, perform this spell first, then choose a relevant spell from Part One to bring you a new job.

You will need

One dark blue candle

Your unemployment card

One crystal

Matches or a lighter

One freezer bag

A freezer or ice box

What you do

Do this spell on a new (dark) moon.

Place the items in the following order: the blue candle at the back; your unemployment card in front of the candle; and the crystal on top of the card.

Light the blue candle and stare into the crystal. Send all your worries about being unemployed into the crystal – let it absorb everything you feel negative about. When you feel ready, say the following words once:

*This is just a phase
in my life
It will pass as quickly
as it came.
I no longer feel disillusioned
about this situation
This crystal absorbs all
my bad luck.*

Allow the candle to burn down. Finally, place your unemployment card in the freezer bag, then secure the bag and leave it overnight in the freezer or ice box. You should soon see an improvement in your employment prospects.

Banishing bad luck

This is one of those wonderfully versatile spells that you can do to banish any form of bad luck you may have experienced – whether you've lost your job, lost the love of your life, had bad luck in your finances, or just feel that things are always going wrong in your life. Try this spell to banish bad luck from your life for ever.

You will need

A silver pen

A piece of black paper

One black feather

One black envelope

Matches or a lighter

A heatproof dish

What you do

Do this spell on a new (dark) moon.

Using the silver pen on the black paper, write down details of whatever bad luck has entered your life, and that you wish to be banished for ever. Write it as though you are writing a letter to 'Mr Bad Luck' and state that you will not tolerate any further bad luck in your life. Get angry if you want to, and let all your feelings pour out – you'll feel so much better for doing this!

Place the black feather with the letter in the envelope, and seal it. Take the envelope outside and set fire to it in the heatproof dish. This will destroy any bad luck that has been sent to you, so that you can now start afresh and look forward to good luck coming your way.

Unlucky in love

We've all had a run of bad luck when it comes to affairs of the
heart. We can't really predict whether our relationships are
going to turn out to be good, or not so good, for us. If you
notice that you keep attracting unsuitable partners, it might
be because you're giving out the wrong signals to them –
signals saying that you don't care how you're treated. If so,
try this little spell to fix matters for ever and banish bad luck
from your love life.

You will need

One sheet of black paper

Scissors

One sheet of pink paper

One black candle

Five pins

Matches or a lighter

What you do

Do this spell on a waning moon.

First of all, cut five small heart shapes out of the black paper – these represent the bad luck you've experienced in your past love life. (It doesn't matter if you're not very good at making paper hearts – the main object is that the black hearts should be smaller than the pink ones. If you fold a piece of paper in two and then cut half a heart shape out, it's easier than trying to create an equal-shaped heart freehand.)

Next, cut five larger heart shapes out of the pink paper – these represent the new good luck that you will have in your love life in the future.

Before you light your black candle, inscribe it with the word 'Banish', using one of the pins. Light the candle and begin to wrap one pink heart around one black heart. Pin both hearts together securely, so that the pink one encloses the black one, which can't escape. Chant the following as you do this:

By the power of love
And the Goddess above
Banish this bad luck
And make me lucky in love.

Leave the pinned hearts out while the candle burns down. This spell will banish the attraction of bad luck in love and send signals out to the universe that you wish to invite only nice partners into your life from now on.

When the candle has burned down, take the five pinned hearts and bury them in your garden or in a flower pot in your home. The reason for this is that, in time, the paper will rot away in the soil and, as it does so, your bad luck in love will go away.

89

A regrettable situation

None of us can predict for certain what will happen when we make a decision, and sometimes – if bad luck is hiding just round the corner – we can regret our actions. This spell is designed for those times when you've done something on the spur of the moment and now wish that you hadn't. This might be something like deciding to chuck in your job, or throwing your partner out. This candle spell will make everything better again.

You will need

Six white candles

Matches or a lighter

What you do

Start this spell on a Monday and repeat it on the next five days.

Try to do this spell at the same time every day for six days. Find a time and place where you will not be disturbed. Light the first candle and say the following words:

I was foolish
Now I am sane
Banish my decision
And restore things again.
A second chance is what
I need
Lord and Lady,
help me, please.

Repeat the ritual on the next five days. After six days something will happen that will make things go back to normal – for example, you will be reinstated in your job (or offered another one), or your partner will call you and you'll make up. I always believe that things happen to us for a reason, so although you may have regretted what you've said or done, it might just be a sign that it's time to move on.

Know your enemy

If you've been having a run of bad luck, it could be that someone is inflicting this bad luck on you. It is important that you know who your enemy is – don't just guess, as this could send the spell out to the wrong person and then it will come back to you. This spell will not harm anyone; it will simply return any bad luck vibes that an enemy is sending out.

You will need

A handful of salt

A mirror with a stand

One black candle

Matches or a lighter

What you do

Do this spell on a Saturday or a waning moon.

First and foremost, you need to protect yourself. To do this, simply cast a circle of salt round you and ask the Goddess to protect you while you perform this spell. Place the mirror behind the black candle, then light the candle. Stare into the flame and chant the following words three times:

By the count of three
I send this back
to thee
Return to your source
And never return
One, Two, Three.

Clap your hands three times above the candle, and then allow it to burn away – don't move the mirror until it has done so. This will return to its original source the bad luck sent to you.

Unlawful arrest

Yes, it can happen. If you, or someone you know, have been arrested for something you haven't done, this spell will ensure that justice will prevail. Please note, however, that it will not work if you have done something unlawful – that is, it doesn't work if you really are guilty!

You will need

One piece of blue paper

A blue pen

One sprig of rosemary

A heatproof dish

Matches or a lighter

What you do

Do this spell on a Saturday or Sunday or a new (dark) moon.

First of all, draw a large pentagram symbol (a five-pointed star within a circle) on the blue paper with your blue pen. Inside the pentagram, draw a picture that represents the reason why you were arrested. This could be a car (if you were suspected of speeding) or a picture of a shop (if you were suspected of shoplifting). Place the sprig of rosemary on top of the picture and close your eyes. Imagine the injustice being rectified and that this moment will soon pass. Visualize for as long as you like, but try not to get angry about the situation.

When you have finished, place the piece of paper and the rosemary in the heatproof dish and set fire to them. This will banish the situation and you will soon see positive results from a bad event.

Legal decision in your favour

This spell will help you if you have been foolish and find
yourself facing court proceedings. But it is not a get-out-
quick spell; you must truly regret what you have done. The
Goddess realizes that people do make mistakes – and we
learn by our mistakes and all deserve a second chance. This
spell will help any legal decisions to go in your favour.

You will need

One silver key

One blue tea-light

Any legal evidence or
documents relating to
the case

A pin

Matches or a lighter

The name of the magistrate in
court, if possible (if you can't
find this out, don't worry)

A piece of paper

A pen

What you do

Try to do this spell on a Thursday.

Place the silver key under the blue tea-light, and put any legal documents relating to your case in front of it. Inscribe the word 'Chance' in the tea-light with the pin, then light it. Say the following words nine times:

I call upon you, Goddess
In my time of need
Look kindly upon me
And grant me the chance
that I seek.
Bring justice and fairness
To my life
Thank you, so mote it be.

Allow the candle to burn down and try not to dwell on the matter any longer. If you have to attend court, write the magistrate's name on a piece of paper and place it in your shoe on the day you go to court. Also take the magically charged key with you, to encourage any decision to go in your favour.

Stop malicious gossip

We all love a good chat about other people, but if that chat turns out to be malicious gossip, it can be hurtful and destructive to the victim. If someone is throwing bad luck at you by spreading malicious gossip about you, try this simple spell to banish the gossip and protect you from the perpetrator.

You will need

A slip of paper with the gossip's name on it

A mixing dish

One red pepper

One green pepper

One strong onion

A knife

A teaspoon of pepper

A freezer or ice box

What you do

Do this spell on a Saturday.

Place the slip of paper in the dish, then chop up the peppers and onion all over it. Next, add the teaspoon of pepper and stir the mixture around. The pepper is a banishing ingredient and the onion acts as a protective ingredient. As you mix, say the following words:

*May your tongue be sour
from your gossip
May your words
return to you
May you realize the pain
you have caused
And harm no one again.*

Place the dish and its contents in the freezer or ice box for 24 hours, then discard the mixture in the wastebin.

Unfair dismissal

Bad luck comes in many disguises, and unfair dismissal may be one of them. If you have lost your job unfairly, you can do this spell to ensure that justice will prevail. Remember: as with any spell for banishing bad luck, don't get angry – get spell casting instead!

You will need

Something relating to the
   dismissal (for example,
   a letter or notice)

Seven of Diamonds playing card

One dark blue candle

Seven silver coins

Matches or a lighter

What you do

You should do this spell on a dark or waning moon.

Place the letter or notice of dismissal underneath the Seven of Diamonds playing card, then put the blue candle on top of this. Place the seven silver coins in a circle round the blue candle. Light the candle, and say the following seven times:

*You know you have
done wrong
And soon you will realize
By the number seven
I return to you the bad luck
you have put upon me*

*And banish you from my
memories.
My life is now better and
justice will overpower your
unfair decision
So mote it be.*

You should soon receive an apology, or news about this situation that will lift your spirits. You might be reinstated, or offered a settlement of some kind and the chance to move on.

Remove a haunting

It's not always the living who inflict bad luck on us. Occasionally a past life can be so unsettled that a spirit will try to upset someone in this world. Known as 'lost souls', such spirits haven't yet managed – or are reluctant – to find their way into the spirit world; they are often disturbed or don't realize they have passed on. If you have been experiencing a run of bad luck and can't pinpoint anyone in the living world who might wish to harm you, try this spell to banish a spirit to his or her rightful home.

You will need

Silver foil

Scissors

A ballpoint pen

One silver candle

Some salt water (two teaspoons of salt to 50ml/2fl oz of water)

A handful of salt

Matches or a lighter

What you do

Do this spell on a waning moon.

Cut a large circle, big enough to place your candle on, out of the silver foil. Write the words 'Go Home' with the ballpoint pen on the foil, then turn it over – this is to reflect the bad luck back where it came from. Place the silver candle on top of the silver foil.

Before you light the candle, take the salt water and sprinkle every room in your house with a few drops. Sit in front of the candle and cast a big circle of salt round you – make sure the circle is not broken while you do this spell. Light your candle and say the following words:

I realize it is not your fault
But it is time for you to
move on now.
Please go through
the light
To your new resting place
Never to return again
Happy journey.

Give yourself five minutes to remain in the protection circle and then you can move out of it. Allow the candle to burn down. Your bad luck should be banished within 24 hours. If you find that you are still experiencing bad luck, or you still feel uneasy, repeat the spell. You may have a spirit who is reluctant to go away and needs some further encouragement from you.

Luck – be it good or bad – has a lot to do with our belief system and how we feel about ourselves. And that doesn't just apply to the living. If you have a spirit who was unlucky in a past life and is hanging around in the living world, that bad luck will rub off on you.

105

Banishing violence

No person should ever be the victim of a violent attack – physical or mental. If you are experiencing violence in your life, put a stop to it now, by using the power within you and the help of the Goddess to protect you and banish violence for good. Please also seek professional help if you are a victim of violence.

You will need

One bag of salt

A piece of paper

A pen

A bowl

Five ice cubes

One black candle

Matches or a lighter

What you do

Do this spell on a Thursday or a waning moon, for protection.

First of all, take your bag of salt and walk round the outside perimeter of your house, trailing a line of salt behind you. (Don't worry if you live in a terraced house or an apartment block – in this case, sprinkle salt all round the inside of your home instead.)

Back inside, write down the name of the person who is being violent to you on the piece of paper. Fold it in four and place it in the bowl. Then put the five ice cubes into the bowl. Light the candle and say the following words, while throwing handfuls of salt on top of the ice cubes:

By the power of the universe
You can harm me no more.
I banish bad luck from
my life
And that includes you
So mote it be.

Allow the candle to burn right down and, when the ice cubes have melted, take the bowl and any remaining candle wax as far away from your home as possible. You should see an immediate improvement in your life.

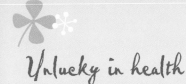

Unlucky in health

Health can be affected by luck – and it's something we all take for granted. If you've suddenly become ill (or you know of someone else who has), try this spell to banish ill health. Please note that this spell merely offers a helping hand, and is not an alternative to seeking medical advice.

You will need

1litre (1¾pt) fresh orange juice

A blender

One teaspoon of cinnamon

One teaspoon of mixed spice

One teaspoon of honey

One peppermint leaf

One bay leaf

Wooden spoon

What you do

Do this spell on a full moon.

Pour the orange juice into a blender, then mix in the cinnamon, mixed spice and honey. Add the peppermint and bay leaves, and stir the mixture with a wooden spoon. Hold your hand over the liquid and say the following words:

*Lady of the Miraculous
Medal
Take this ill health away
from me/
[other person's name]
Absorb this illness
So that it may never return.*

*By the power of this potion
Good health will return
So mote it be.*

Assuming that the spell is for you, pour yourself one glass of your health potion. As you sip the mixture, imagine a warm orange glow entering your body. Visualize it destroying any illness within your body as you continue to sip it. Pour yourself another glass in the evening. Within three days you should feel better. (If you are making the potion for someone else, get them to take it as described above.)

Fertility bad luck

Fertility difficulties are not always due to a medical problem. They can sometimes be put down to other causes – stress, trying too hard, or even a run of bad luck in other areas of your life. So long as you have no medical reason why you can't conceive, this candle spell should banish all of the above, making way for conception to take place.

You will need

One dark blue candle

Matches or a lighter

One silver candle

One pink candle

One light blue candle

What you do

Do this candle spell every time there's a full moon.

First, light the dark blue candle and say:

*By the power of light
Banish any problems that
have prevented me from
becoming a mother.*

Next, light the silver candle and say:

*By the power of the
silver moon
Carry my message to
the universe.*

Next, light the pink and the blue candles and say:

*By the power of the infant
I call upon you to
come to me
You will be a strong and
healthy child,
Motherhood awaits me.*

Allow the candles to burn down. Make love to your partner this night. If you haven't conceived by the same time the following month, repeat the spell. This spell can take a while to kick in, so do persevere, because it should work.

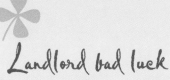

Landlord bad luck

As I pointed out earlier in this book, some people can purposely inflict bad luck on you by their actions. If you are having problems with a power-crazed landlord (yes, there are some out there), try this spell to keep him at bay.

You will need

A photocopy of something relating to the landlord or property (for example, a rent book or a contract)

A piece of paper

A pen

One black candle

Matches or a lighter

One matchstick

A heatproof dish

What you do

Do this spell on a waning moon.

First and foremost, make sure you are using a photocopy of the item relating to your landlord, because you have to burn it to make this banishing spell work.

Draw a stick figure of your landlord on a small piece of paper. Place the copy of your document and the stick figure under the black candle, then light the candle. Chant the following words three times:

By the power of this spell
I banish you [name of landlord]
You will no longer bring bad luck to my home
You will no longer upset me.
By the power of Karma and the power of three
All you've done will come back to thee.

Just before the candle burns down, light the matchstick and blow it out. Using the burned end of the matchstick, draw a charcoal cross through the stickman. Set fire to the copy of your document and the picture of the stickman in the heatproof dish, then blow out the candle. You should soon see an improvement in relations with your landlord – or, at the very least, he will not bother you again.

Financial bad luck

We all have times in our lives when we have more money going out than coming in. This is a spell designed for general use when you discover that you are having endless amounts of bad luck financially. It could be that you simply don't have enough money to see you through to your next pay day, or that you are facing the prospect of bankruptcy. Do this spell to banish financial bad luck, then go back to Part One and do the spell for Financial Luck (see pages 30–33).

You will need

A photocopy of a recent bank statement

A black pen

A photocopy of a recent bill

Glue

A handful of red glitter

One dark blue candle

Matches or a lighter

A photocopy of a blank cheque from your cheque book

A handful of silver glitter

What you do

Do this spell on a new (dark) moon.

Take the photocopy of your recent bank statement and cross out any amounts that show you are in debt, changing them to a credit with a black pen. Next, take the photocopy of a recent bill and write across it in big black letters the word 'paid'. Place these two photocopies on a table and paste some glue all over them. Next, sprinkle red glitter over both copies. Put the blue candle on top of the copies and light it. Say the following words:

By the time this spell is done
My finances will improve.
I banish all debt to
the universe
May you help in my quest to
remove these financial
obstacles from my life.

Allow the candle to burn down. Next, take the photocopy of the blank cheque and write the following in the space where you normally write the amount in words: 'enough

money for my needs'. Sign the cheque. Place it on top of the copies of your bill and bank statement. Paste a small amount of glue over the cheque, then sprinkle the silver glitter on top and say the following words:

By the power of this spell
I banish poverty
from my life
Leaving only room for
prosperity to flourish.
This is my quest,
so mote it be.

Leave the pile undisturbed for 24 hours to enable the message to be carried to the universe. Tidy your spell away and keep the photocopied documents, cheque and glitter together in your financial folder. You should notice an improvement in your finances within 28 days.

Specific bad luck

There might be a specific area of your life where you have had a run of bad luck, and which I haven't covered in this book. You can adapt most spells to suit your own situation, but if there is a subject that I haven't touched upon, this spell is designed to cover every kind of bad luck.

You will need

A piece of paper

A pen

One black candle

Matches or a lighter

A heatproof dish

What you do

Do this spell on a waning or new (dark) moon.

First and foremost, concentrate on the situation from which you wish to banish bad luck. Write it down on the piece of paper. Write as much as you can about the situation – it could be that you feel your whole life has been plagued by bad luck, with the result that you feel a failure at everything you do. If so, write it down, including as much or as little detail as you like.

Light the black candle, and say the following words:

Lord and Lady I call upon you to banish [name the situation] From me here and now. Please grant my wish and make my life lucky again Banish this time to the past And may it never return to me.

When the candle has burned halfway down, set fire to the piece of paper and drop it into the heatproof dish. Carry the ashes outside and allow the wind to take them away. Imagine your worries being swept away with the wind – never again to return.

Retracting a spell

The reason why I emphasize that you should always think carefully about what you are doing before you perform any spell is because spells *do* work! Sometimes we may regret casting a spell and wish that we hadn't done it. For example, you might perform a spell to find a new job because your boss has upset you, only to have him apologize the following day and offer you a pay rise. If you do a spell and later regret it, don't panic, for you can retract the spell using a white candle.

You will need

One white candle

Matches or a lighter

What you do

You can do this spell at any time.

Light the white candle and stare into the flame. Think about the spell that you performed and why you now wish to retract it. Keep looking into the flame and say the following words three times:

By the power of three
I ask that you, Goddess,
may retract
And bring me back to
where I started.
Please grant my wish
forthwith
Thank you, so mote it be.

When you say these words, you should notice the flame of the candle flicker. Imagine that you are sending out a brilliant white light to capture the spell before it enters the universe. Visualize it cupping the original spell that you performed in its hands and bringing it back home. Allow the candle to burn down safely.

Your spell will now be retracted and won't reach its destination. The Goddess has done you a favour, so by way of thanks make her a gift of nature (for example, plant a packet of seeds, a flower or a small tree, or donate some money to charity).

Don't be complacent and assume that the Goddess will bail you out every time you do a spell – she won't. If you make a habit of spell casting just for the fun of it, she may let the spell reach its destination in order to make you think about what you did!

123

Conclusion

We look enviously at some people and think they are always lucky. And you know what? They probably are! 'So why not me?' I hear you ask. Well, the answer is quite simple really. In every area of our lives we are either lucky or unlucky, depending on our state of mind and what it is that we believe to be true.

You can of course enhance your life by casting spells to either banish or increase luck, but if you already believe that you are a lucky person, you will probably attract good luck in every area of your life. Conversely, if you believe you are the unluckiest person on the planet, you will have to work twice as hard to bring good luck into your life.

Different cultures have different rituals that they perform in a bid to become lucky or avoid bad luck. For example, some people won't walk under a ladder for fear of bringing bad luck into their lives. Others believe that if a black cat walks past you, it will bring good luck. Finding something rare, such as a four-leafed clover, is widely thought to bring you enormous good luck. But the reality is that you already *are* lucky.

You're lucky to be alive right now, reading this book – it's amazing how we take for granted the complicated process of our heart working properly to keep us alive. You're lucky to be able to wake up in the morning to a fresh day, full of new opportunities. You're lucky to be able to see the beauty in this world. So don't spend time convincing yourself that you're unlucky, because you're not.

You will experience what is termed 'bad luck' from time to time throughout your entire life – no spell will work for ever, I'm afraid. But, armed with this book and the perception that a run of bad luck is a challenge, you'll be well equipped to banish any bad luck and increase the good luck in your life.

We have now come to the end of this little cauldron of good luck spells. I hope you have enjoyed working with this book as much as I have enjoyed writing it. May you always be lucky in life, because you deserve it, don't you?

Index

Executive Editor *Brenda Rosen*
Managing Editor *Clare Churly*
Executive Art Editor *Sally Bond*
Designer *Pia Hietarinta for Cobalt id*
Illustrator *Arlene Adams*
Senior Production Controller *Ian Paton*